AF107561

Published By Adam Gilbin

@ Brent Morin

Sirtfood Diet for Beginners: A Step-by-step Guide

to Cleanse Your Body Naturally

All Right RESERVED

ISBN 978-87-94477-25-3

TABLE OF CONTENTS

Chocolate Granola 1

Chocolate Waffles 3

Banana Smoothie With Berries 6

Matcha Green Tea Smoothie 7

Green Juice 9

Strawberry Chocolate Shakes 11

Quinoa Breakfast With Chocolate And Coconut 12

Spread With Tomatoes 13

Aromatic Chicken Breast With Kale, Red Onions And A Tomato & Chili Salsa 15

Shrimp Stir-Fry With Buckwheat Noodles 18

Sirtfood Green Juice 21

Grilled Chicken With Kale And Buckwheat Salad 24

Bolognese With Zoodles 27

Potato Bites 29

Rosemary Squash Dip 30

Mushroom Scramble 31

Date And Walnut Porridge 32

Vegan Rice Pudding 34

Cinnamon Scented Quinoa Breakfast 36

Chocolate Granola 38

Melon Smoothie 41

Date And Walnut Porridge 42

Avocado Eggs With Toast 43

Broccolini With Pine Nuts And Garlic 46

Olive Oil, Caramelized Onion, And Sage Mashed Sweet Potatoes 48

Maple Glazed Green Beans With Toasted Quinoa 51

Sirtburger With Sweet Potato Buns 53

Simple Couscous Salad 56

Date & Walnut Cinnamon Bites 58

Red Chicory, Pear & Hazelnut Salad 59

Easy Grilled Salmon 61

Kidney Bean Mole With Potato Backed 64

Omelet-Sirtfood 67

Baked Breast Chicken With Walnut And Parsley Pesto And Red Onion Salad 69

Honey, Garlic And Chilli Oven-Roasted Squash 72

Homemade Roasted Celery Hummus 74

Kale Scramble 76

Eggs With Kale 78

Green Smoothie With Berries 80

Green Smoothie With Grapefruit 81

Cacao Protein Shake 82

Power Green Smoothie 84

Sour Cherry Skyr Bowl With Kiwi And Raspberry 85

Beetroot Bread With Nasturtium 87

Zebra Bread With Cream Cheese 89

Strawberry Buckwheat Tabbouleh 91

Sirtfood Green Juice 93

Turmeric Chicken & Kale Salad With Honey Lime Dressing 95

Buckwheat Noodles With Chicken Kale 99

Stir-Fry With Buckwheat Noodles 103

Baked Salmon Salad With Creamy Mint Dressing-Sirtfood Recipes 106

Chargrilled Beef With A Red Wine Jus, Onion Rings, Garlic Kale And Herb Roasted Potatoes 109

Kale And Blackcurrant Smoothie................................... 113

Eggplant Salsa.. 114

Carrots And Cauliflower Spread 116

Italian Veggie Salsa.. 118

Smoked Salmon Omelet.. 119

Cheesy Baked Eggs 121

Oatmeal Banana Pancakes With Walnuts..................... 123

Buckwheat And Strawberries Salad 124

Miso And Sesame Glazed Tofu With Ginger And Chili Stir-Fried Greens 125

Buckwheat Noodles... 130

Baked Oatmeal 133

Choc Chip Granola... 135

Caramelized Cauliflower 137

Colorado Potato Hash 139

Chocolate Granola

Ingredients:

- 1/8 teaspoon salt
- 2 cups gluten-free rolled oats
- ¼ cup unsweetened coconut flakes
- 2 tablespoons chia seeds
- ¼ cup cacao powder
- ¼ cup maple syrup
- 2 tablespoons coconut oil, melted
- ½ teaspoon vanilla extract
- 2 tablespoons unsweetened dark chocolate, chopped finely

Directions:

1. Preheat your oven to 300°F. Line a medium baking sheet with parchment paper.
2. In a medium pan, add the cacao powder, maple syrup, coconut oil, vanilla extract and salt and mix well.
3. Now, place pan over medium heat and cook for about 2-3 minutes or until thick and syrupy, stirring continuously.
4. Remove the pan of mixture from the heat and set aside. In a large bowl, add the oats, coconut and chia seeds and mix well.
5. Add the syrup mixture and mix until well combined.
6. Transfer the granola mixture onto a prepared baking sheet and spread in an even layer.
7. Bake for approximately 35 minutes. Remove the baking sheet from oven and set aside for about 1 hour.
8. Add the chocolate pieces and stir to combine.
9. Serve immediately.

Chocolate Waffles

Ingredients:

- ¼ teaspoons kosher salt
- 2 large eggs
- ½ cup coconut oil, melted
- ¼ cup dark brown sugar
- 2 teaspoons vanilla extract
- 2 ounces unsweetened dark chocolate, chopped roughly
- 2 cups unsweetened almond milk
- 1 tablespoon fresh lemon juice
- 1 cup buckwheat flour
- ½ cup cacao powder

- ¼ cup flaxseed meal

- 1 teaspoon baking soda

- 1 teaspoon baking powder

Directions:

1. In a bowl, add the almond milk and lemon juice and mix well.
2. Set aside for about 10 minutes. In a bowl, place buckwheat flour, cacao powder, flaxseed meal, baking soda, baking powder and salt and mix well. In the bowl of almond milk mixture, place the eggs, coconut oil, brown sugar and vanilla extract and beat until smooth.
3. Now, place the flour mixture and beat until smooth.
4. Gently, fold in the chocolate pieces. Preheat the waffle iron and then grease it.

5. Place the desired amount of the mixture into the preheated waffle iron and cook for about 3 minutes or until golden brown.
6. Repeat with the remaining mixture. Serve warm.

Banana Smoothie With Berries

Ingredients:

- 1 cup blueberries

- 2 tbsp. natural yogurt

- 1 cup milk (or soy/almond or rice milk)

- 1 banana

- 1 cup blackberries

Directions:

1. Add all to a blender and process until smooth.
2. Serve immediately or slightly chilled.

Matcha Green Tea Smoothie

Ingredients:

- 1 ½ cups milk
- 4-5 ice cubes
- 2 tsp honey
- 2 bananas
- 2 tsp Matcha green tea powder
- 1/2 tsp vanilla bean (paste or scraped from a vanilla bean pod)

Directions:

1. Add all Ingredients::except the Matcha to a blender. Blend until smooth. (Make sure you have an ice-crusher blender, otherwise, leave out the ice and add later)

2. When ready to serve, add the matcha and stir well.
3. Let the Matcha dissolve for a few minutes before you serve

Green Juice

Ingredients:

- Rocket o2ne cup (roughly chopped)
- Juice of a 1 lemon
- Matcha green tea half teaspoon
- Green apple half
- Ginger 1 inch
- Celery 3 sticks
- Parsley 1 ounce
- Kale 1 ¼ cups

Directions:

1. Add the rocket, apple, parsley, kale, ginger, and celery to your juicer and blend. Transfer

the mixture into your glass, and squeeze in the lemon juice.
2. Add the green tea powder to the juice, then stir before you drink.

Strawberry Chocolate Shakes

Ingredients:

- Vanilla extract half teaspoon
- Water 2cup
- Cacao powder 2 tablespoon
- Frozen strawberries 2 cup
- Baby arugula 2 ounce
- Avocado 1

Directions:

1. Move all your Ingredients::into a food processor and blitz until you get a creamy and smooth texture.
2. You may add some ice if you want the shakes to be thicker. Serve immediately!

Quinoa Breakfast With Chocolate And Coconut

Ingredients:

- 1 tbsp cocoa powder
- salt
- walnuts (to taste)
- dark chocolate (to taste)
- coconut flakes (to taste)
- fruit (at will)
- 75 g quinoa
- 1 apple
- 150 ml of coconut milk
- 2 tsp honey
- 2 tbsp linseed

Directions:

1. Rinse the quinoa in a colander under hot water. Then put 150 ml of water in a saucepan and bring to the boil.
2. Cover and simmer for about 15 minutes. Meanwhile, cut the apple into cubes or slices.
3. Add coconut milk, honey, flaxseed, cocoa powder and salt to the quinoa, heat over low heat and stir well.
4. Divide the quinoa breakfast into 2 small bowls and garnish with nuts, chocolate, coconut flakes and fruit as desired.

Spread With Tomatoes

Ingredients:

- 3 tbsp rapeseed oil
- salt
- pepper

- 3 stems basil

- 4 slices oat bread

- 100 g dried tomato in oil

- 100 g sunflower seeds

Directions:

1. Drain the tomatoes slightly and cut roughly. Then place in a tall container and puree together with 90 g sunflower seeds, rapeseed oil and 3–4 tablespoons of water. Then season with salt and pepper.
2. Wash the basil, shake dry and finely chop the leaves. Add 3/4 of the basil to the tomato spread and stir in.
3. Spread tomato spread on four slices of oat bread. Sprinkle with the remaining sunflower seeds and basil and serve.

Aromatic Chicken Breast With Kale, Red Onions And A Tomato & Chili Salsa

Ingredients:

Ingredients:

- 1/8 cup of red onion (sliced)
- 1/3 cup of buckwheat
- 1/4-pound of chicken breast (skinless & boneless)
- 3/4 cup of kale (chopped)
- 3 teaspoons of ground turmeric
- 1/4 lemon juice
- 2 teaspoon of fresh ginger (chopped)
- 2 tablespoon of extra-virgin olive oil

For the salsa:

- 1/4 lemon juice

- 2 Thai chili (finely chopped)

- 2 tablespoon capers (finely chopped)

- 2 medium tomato

- 3 tablespoons parsley (finely chopped)

Directions:

1. To prepare the salsa, remove the eye from the tomato and slice it very finely, ensuring the liquid stays as large as possible.
2. Mix the capers, chili, lemon juice and parsley together.
3. You can put it all in a clean blender, but the final outcome might be a little different.
4. Preheat the oven to 425 degrees Fahrenheit. In one teaspoon of turmeric, the lemon juice and a little oil, marinate the chicken breast. Leave for about five to ten minutes.

5. Heat the ovenproof frying pan till heat is high, then add the marinated chicken to each side for a minute, until it appears pale golden, then move to the oven (ensure to place on a baking tray if it is not ovenproof) for eight to ten minutes, or until well cooked.
6. Take out from the oven, gently cover with foil, and leave for five minutes before serving it.
7. In the meantime, in a steamer cook kale for about five minutes.
8. Fry the ginger and the red onions in some little oil, until it becomes soft but also not browned, and then add the cooked kale and fry for some additional minute.
9. Cook the buckwheat with the remaining turmeric teaspoon according to product Directions:. Serve together with the vegetables, salsa and chicken.

Shrimp Stir-Fry With Buckwheat Noodles

Ingredients:

Ingredients:

- 1/8 cup of red onions (sliced)
- 1/3-pound of shelled raw jumbo shrimp (deveined)
- 2 teaspoon of fresh ginger (finely chopped)
- 3/4 cup of kale (roughly chopped)
- 2 teaspoons of tamari (or soy sauce, for gluten-free)
- 1 cup of chicken stock
- 2 teaspoons of extra-virgin olive oil
- 1 cup of green beans (chopped)
- 3 garlic cloves (finely chopped)

- 2 Thai chili (finely chopped)

- 4-ounces of soba (buckwheat noodles)

- 1 cup of celery including leaves (trimmed & sliced, with leaves put separately)

Directions:

1. Heat up a large clean frying pan over high heat, in one teaspoon of the oil and one teaspoon of the tamari, cook the shrimp for about two to three minutes.
2. You should then transfer the shrimp to a dish. Using a paper towel carefully wipe out the pan. You'll use again.
3. In boiling water cook the noodles for five to eight minutes or as instructed on the package. Remove water and then put aside.
4. Afterwards, fry the chili, red onion, ginger, celery (don't include leaves), kale, green beans and garlic in the rest of the tamari and

oil over medium to high heat for approximately two to three mins.
5. Having done that, add the stock and then bring to a boil also simmer for one to two mins, until the vegetables are cooked but remain crunchy.
6. Add the noodles, celery leaves and the shrimp to the pan, then bring back to a boil, then take away from the heat and then serve.

Sirtfood Green Juice

Ingredients:

- 2 to 3 large celery stalks (5 1/2 ounces or 150g), including leaves

- 1/2 medium green apple

- 1/2 to 1-inch (1 to 2.5 cm) piece of fresh ginger

- Juice of 1/2 lemon

- 2 large handfuls (about 2 1/2 ounces or 75g)

- Kale a large handful (1 ounce or 30g) arugula

- A very small handful (about 1/4 ounce or 5g) flat-leaf parsley

- 1/2 level teaspoon matcha powder

Directions:

1. Mix the greens (kale, arugula, and parsley) together, then juice them.
2. We find that juicers can really differ in their efficiency at juicing leafy vegetables, and you may need to rejuice the remnants before moving on to the other Ingredients:.
3. The goal is to end up with about 2 fluid ounces or close to 1/4 cup (50ml) of juice from the greens.
4. Now juice the celery, apple, and ginger. You can peel the lemon and put it through the juicer as well, but we find it much easier to simply squeeze the lemon by hand into the juice.
5. By this stage, you should have around 1 cup (250ml) of juice in total, perhaps slightly more.
   It is only when the juice is made and ready to serve that you add the matcha.

6. Pour a small amount of the juice into a glass, then add the matcha and stir vigorously with a fork or teaspoon.
7. Once the matcha is dissolved, add the remainder of the juice.
8. Give it a final stir, then your juice is ready to drink. Feel free to top up with plain water, according to taste.

Grilled Chicken With Kale And Buckwheat Salad

Ingredients:

- 4 cups chopped kale
- 1 cup cooked buckwheat
- 1/4 cup chopped walnuts
- 1 tbsp olive oil
- 2 boneless, skinless chicken breasts
- 1/4 cup soy sauce
- 2 tbsp honey
- 1 green tea bag
- Salt and pepper to taste

Directions:

1. In a bowl, mix together the soy sauce, honey, and the contents of the green tea bag.

2. Place the chicken breasts in a shallow dish or resealable bag and pour the marinade over them, making sure they are evenly coated.
3. Cover the dish or seal the bag and let the chicken marinate in the refrigerator for at least 30 minutes, or up to 2 hours.
4. Heat a grill pan or outdoor grill over medium-high heat.
5. Remove the chicken breasts from the marinade and discard the marinade.
6. Season the chicken breasts with salt and pepper.
7. Grill the chicken for 6-8 minutes per side, or until cooked through and the internal temperature reaches 165°F.
8. While the chicken is cooking, prepare the salad. In a large bowl, combine the chopped kale, cooked buckwheat, and chopped walnuts.

9. Drizzle the olive oil over the salad and toss to coat evenly.
10. Divide the salad onto two plates and top each with a grilled chicken breast.
11. Serve and enjoy!

Bolognese With Zoodles

Ingredients:

- 1/2 teaspoon salt

- 1/4 teaspoon black pepper

- 2 cups diced canned tomatoes

- 1 cup beef or chicken broth

- 2 cups zucchini noodles (zoodles)

- 1 pound lean ground beef

- 1 tablespoon olive oil

- 1 large onion, finely chopped

- 4 garlic cloves, minced

- 1/2 teaspoon dried basil

- 1/2 teaspoon dried oregano

- 1/2 teaspoon dried thyme

Directions:

1. In a large skillet, heat the olive oil over medium-high heat. Add the ground beef and cook until browned, about 5-7 minutes.
2. Add the onion and garlic to the skillet and cook until the onion is translucent, about 5 minutes.
3. Add the basil, oregano, thyme, salt, and black pepper to the skillet and stir to combine.
4. Add the diced tomatoes and broth to the skillet and bring to a simmer. Reduce the heat to low and let the sauce simmer for 20-25 minutes, or until it has thickened.
5. While the sauce is simmering, prepare the zucchini noodles. You can use a spiralizer or a vegetable peeler to make the zoodles.
6. Once the sauce is done simmering, divide the zoodles among 4 plates and spoon the sauce over the top.

Potato Bites

Ingredients:

- 2 bacon slices, already cooked and crumbled
- 1 small avocado, pitted and cubed
- 1 potato, sliced
- Cooking spray

Directions:

1. Spread potato slices on a lined baking sheet, spray with cooking oil, introduce in the oven at 350 degrees F, bake for 20 minutes, arrange on a platter, top each slice with avocado and crumbled bacon and serve as a snack.
2. Enjoy!

Rosemary Squash Dip

Ingredients:

- 2 tbsps. coconut milk
- 2 tsps. rosemary, dried
- Black pepper to the taste
- 1 c. butternut squash, peeled and cubed
- 1 tbsp. water
- Cooking spray

Directions:

1. Spread squash cubes on a lined baking sheet, spray some cooking oil, introduce in the oven, bake at 365 degrees F for 40 minutes, transfer to your blender, add water, milk, rosemary and black pepper, pulse well, divide into small bowls and serveEnjoy!

Mushroom Scramble

Ingredients:

- 2 teaspoons olive oil (extra virgin)
- 1 bird's eye chili, sliced (remove seeds if you prefer less burn)
- Button mushrooms sliced up—just a handful or two
- 1/3 cup of parsley, chopped
- 4 eggs
- 2 teaspoons turmeric (ground)
- 3 teaspoons curry powder
- 2/3 cup chopped kale

Directions:

1. Combine the turmeric and curry powder in a small bowl. Add a small amount of water and mix until it creates a paste
2. In a pot, steam your kale for just a few minutes—no more than 3
3. Heat the oil up on medium in a frying pan. Then, sauté the mushroom slices and the pepper slices. Wait for the mushrooms to start to soften.
4. Then, crack the eggs into the pan and mix with the spice paste. Cook the whole thing over medium heat for a minute and then mix in the kale.
5. Cook for another minute or until eggs are fully cooked. Then add the parsley to the pan, mix together to combine, and serve.

Date And Walnut Porridge

Ingredients:

- 8 chopped cup walnut halves
- 70 g buckwheat flakes
- 400 mL of milk of any kind (cow, goat, soy, almond, coconut, etc.)
- 2 Medjool dates
- 100 g strawberries, washed, hulled, and chopped

Directions:

Add the milk into a pot with the dates.

Slowly heat it and then add in the buckwheat.

Continue to cook until the porridge is the right consistency for you.

Add in the walnuts and top with strawberries. Serve immediately.

Vegan Rice Pudding

Ingredients:

- 1/8 teaspoon ground cardamom
- ¼ cup sugar
- 1/8 teaspoon pure almond extract
- 1-quart vanilla nondairy milk
- ½ teaspoons ground cinnamon
- 1 cup rinsed basmati
- 1 teaspoon pure vanilla extract

Directions:

1. Measure all the Ingredients::into a saucepan and stir well to combine.
2. Bring to a boil over medium-high heat.

3. Once boiling, reduce heat to low and simmer, stirring very frequently, about 15–20 minutes.
4. Remove from heat and cold.
5. Serve sprinkled with additional ground cinnamon if desired.

Cinnamon Scented Quinoa Breakfast

Ingredients:

- Maple syrup for topping
- 2 cinnamon sticks
- 1 cup quinoa
- Chopped walnuts for topping
- 1 ½ cup water

Directions:

1. Add the quinoa to a bowl and wash it in several changes of water until the water is clear.
2. When washing quinoa, rub grains and allow them to settle before you pour off the water.
3. Use a large fine-mesh sieve to drain the quinoa.

4. Prepare your pressure cooker with a trivet and steaming basket.
5. Place the quinoa and the cinnamon sticks in the basket and pour in the water.
6. Close and lock the lid.
7. Cook at high pressure for 6 minutes. When the cooking time is up, release the pressure using the quick-release method.
8. Fluff the quinoa with a fork and remove the cinnamon sticks.
9. Divide the cooked quinoa among serving bowls and top with maple syrup and chopped walnuts.

Chocolate Granola

Ingredients:

- 2 teaspoon fine sea salt
- 1/2 cup melted coconut oil
- 1/2 cup maple syrup
- 3 teaspoons vanilla extract
- 1/2 cup semisweet chocolate chips (optional)
- 5 cups old-fashioned oats
- 2 cup slivered almonds (or your preferred nuts)
- 1/3 cup unsweetened cocoa powder
- 1/2 cup shredded coconut (or 2/3 cup unsweetened flaked coconut)

Directions:

1. Heat the oven to 350 degrees. Line a large baking sheet and set it aside with parchment paper.
2. Stir the oats, almonds, cocoa powder, and sea salt together in a large bowl and mix until evenly mixed.
3. Stir together the melted coconut oil, vanilla extract, and maple syrup in a separate mixing cup, until mixed.
4. Pour the coconut oil mixture into the oats mixture and whisk until evenly mixed.
5. On the prepared baking sheet, spread the granola out evenly. Bake, stirring once halfway through, for twenty minutes.
6. Then remove it from the oven, add a good stir to the mixture, then sprinkle the coconut on top evenly. Bake until the granola is lightly toasted and golden.

7. Remove and transfer the baking sheet from the oven to a wire baking rack. Let the granola cool until it reaches room temperature.
8. Then stir in the chocolate chips or/and any other add-ins.
9. Serve immediately, or place it in an airtight jar for up to 1 month at room temperature.

Melon Smoothie

Ingredients:

- 1 lime, juiced
- 2 tablespoons sugar
- ¼ cantaloupe peeled, seeded, and cubed
- ¼ honeydew melon peeled, seeded, and cubed

Directions:

1. In a blender, combine cantaloupe, honeydew, lime juice, and sugar. Blend until smooth. Pour into glasses and serve.

Date And Walnut Porridge

Ingredients:

- 35 g Buckwheat chips
- 1 tsp. Pecan spread or four cleaved pecan parts
- 50 g Strawberries, hulled
- 200 ml Milk or without dairy elective
- 1 Medjool date, hacked

Directions:

1. Spot the milk and time. In a dish, heat tenderly; at that time, include the buckwheat chips and cook until the porridge is your ideal consistency.
2. Mix In the pecan margarine or pecans, top with the strawberries, and serve.

Avocado Eggs With Toast

Ingredients:

- ¼ teaspoon salt, separated
- ¼ teaspoon ground pepper, separated
- 5 tablespoons salsa
- 2 avocado
- 4 cuts entire wheat sandwich bread
- 3 tablespoons avocado oil
- 5 medium eggs

Directions:

1. Preheat stove to 375 degrees F. Coat an enormous rimmed preparing sheet with cooking splash.

2. Split avocado and strip. Cut the great distance into 1/4-inch-thick cuts, so you've got traverse the whole length of the avocado with the gap from Hell.
3. Separate the four cuts nearest to either side of the opening and, therefore, the external cuts; put In a safe spot.
4. Utilizing a baked good brush, delicately cover the two sides of every cut of bread with oil.
5. Cut a bit out of the focus of every bread cut, looking like an avocado cut.
6. Move the dough and slice out bread pieces to the readied heating sheet. Spot the external avocado cuts In the gaps of the bread.
7. Split an egg over all of the avocado cuts In the dough.
8. Sprinkle the eggs with 1/8 teaspoon salt and 1/8 teaspoon pepper.
9. Every each egg with one among the avocado cuts taken from the part nearest to Hell with a

gap in them, uncovering the egg. Sprinkle the avocado with the staying 1/8 teaspoon salt and 1/8 teaspoon pepper.

10. Prepare until the toast has seared in spots, and therefore the eggs are simply set 10 to 12 minutes. Top with salsa, whenever wanted. Present with the cut-out bread pieces.

Broccolini With Pine Nuts And Garlic

Ingredients:

- 16 garlic cloves thinly sliced

- 1/2 Tsp salt

- 1/4 Tsp freshly ground black pepper

- 2 pounds broccolini

- 1/3 cup pine nuts

- 6 Tbl   extra virgin olive oil

Directions:

1. Bring a large pot of salted water to a boil. Add the broccolini, cover, return to a boil and cook 3 minutes. Drain and rinse the broccolini under cold water to stop the cooking process; drain again.

2. Heat a large nonstick skillet over medium heat.
3. Add the pine nuts and cook, shaking pan often, until lightly browned, 3 to 5 minutes; transfer to a bowl.
4. Return skillet to the heat and add 3 tablespoons oil and half the garlic.
5. Cook the garlic, stirring occasionally, until just starting to brown slightly, 1 to 2 minutes.
6. Add half of the broccolini and half of the pine nuts; cook, tossing, until hot, 2 to 3 minutes.
7. Season with 1/4 teaspoon salt and 1/8 teaspoon pepper; transfer to a bowl and repeat with remaining Ingredients: : Serve hot.

Olive Oil, Caramelized Onion, And Sage Mashed Sweet Potatoes

Ingredients:

- 4-5 fresh sage leaves, thinly sliced crosswise

- 1 Tsp coarse sea salt

- 7-8 cranks freshly ground black pepper

- 1-2 Tsp quality extra virgin olive oil, for drizzling

- 2 large, orange fleshed sweet potatoes, scrubbed, peeled and diced (about 4 cups diced)

- 4 Tbl extra virgin olive oil, divided (regular olive oil is fine for cooking)

- 1 large yellow onion, thinly sliced

- 2 Tbl light brown sugar

Directions:

1. Place diced potatoes in a medium saucepan. Cover with cold water. Bring to a boil and cook until tender when pierced with a fork. Drain immediately.
2. Meanwhile, heat 2 tablespoons extra virgin olive oil in a large skillet over medium-low heat.
3. Add sliced onions and brown sugar; stir occasionally, until the onions caramelize and turn a deep golden brown, about 10-12 minutes.
4. In a small skillet over medium heat, add remaining 2 tablespoons extra virgin olive oil.
5. Add sliced sage leaves and saute until lightly crisp. Remove from heat.
6. Using a hand-held potato masher or an electric mixer, mash potatoes to desired consistency.

7. Add the caramelized onions and the crisp sage leaves in extra virgin olive oil to the potatoes.
8. Add coarse sea salt and freshly ground black pepper. Stir until well blended.
9. Drizzle with extra virgin olive oil and sprinkle with a little sea salt before serving.

Maple Glazed Green Beans With Toasted Quinoa

Ingredients:

- 2 Tbl   extra virgin olive oil
- 1/4 cup maple syrup
- 1/4 Tsp salt
- Pinch of red pepper flakes
- 1/4 cup Alter Eco Rainbow Quinoa
- 1/4 cup water
- 1 pound French haricot verts or thin green beans

Directions:

1. Rinse quinoa under cold water until runs clear. Place quinoa in a large skillet, over medium heat, stir until dry. 1 minute.

2. Turn heat to medium-high, stir until the grains start to brown and a nutty smell arises. Remove from pan. Set aside.
3. Place water in a large skillet, heat to a boil. Add green beans, cover, reduce heat to medium-low, steam 3-minutes or until slightly under done. Pour off water.
4. Add   extra virgin olive oil, stir for 30 seconds to coat green beans then add maple syrup, red pepper, and salt.
5. Turn heat to high for 1-2 minute, stirring constantly, until green beans are glazed with caramelized maple syrup. Adjust time for cooking if green beans are large.
6. Transfer to green beans to a serving dish and sprinkle with toasted quinoa.

Sirtburger With Sweet Potato Buns

Ingredients:

- Some radicchio
- 1 red onion
- A little avocado
- Some tomato
- Dijon mustard
- 1 teaspoon paprika powder, noble sweet
- salt and pepper
- 1 pickle
- 1 sweet potato as round as possible
- 100 to 150g minced meat
- Some arugula

- Virgin olive oil

Directions:

1. At the beginning, preheat the oven to 250 ° C top / bottom heat.
2. Now we can start: Peel the sweet potato and cut into approx. 1 cm thick slices.
3. Then mix the paprika powder, salt, pepper and a bit of the olive oil and brush the sweet potato slices with it.
4. Then place these on a baking sheet lined with baking paper. Now the "buns" are pushed into the oven and baked for about 25 minutes.
5. Remember that the "buns" have to cool down a bit, so it doesn't do any harm to plan a little more time.
6. In the meantime, we can prepare the burger "patties". These are formed from the minced meat. It is best to use a burger press so that the "patties" keep their shape in the

pan. Then fry them briefly on both sides in olive oil.
7. Then put them in the oven together with an ovenproof pan / dish; at 120 ° C top / bottom heat until they reach the desired cooking point.
8. Meanwhile, the radicchio is cut into very thin strips and the onion into rings. We need pickles, avocados and tomatoes in thin slices. The rocket just needs to be washed.
9. Now we can finally top our sweet potato bun. We'll start with the salad and the pattie.
10. Put a little Dijon mustard on top and cover everything with the remaining Ingredients:.
11. A second bun is put on top as the last and everything is refined with a few coarse sea salt flakes. A skewer can help hold the burger together.

Simple Couscous Salad

Ingredients:

- 1 red onion
- 50g tomato paste
- 4 tablespoons of oil
- salt
- lemon juice
- 250g couscous
- 2 pointed peppers, red
- ½ bunch of parsley
- Hot chili paste (e.g. harissa)

Directions:

1. First cook the couscous, just follow the Directions:on the packet. Maybe let it cook a little less, then it won't be so mushy.
2. In the meantime, we can cut the bell pepper into small cubes and the red onion into rings. We need the parsley finely chopped, it doesn't necessarily have to be very fine, depending on taste.
3. When the couscous is ready, we mix it with all the other Ingredients:. Salt, lemon juice, and chilli can be added as desired.
4. A little tip: Even after 2 days in the refrigerator, it still tastes good.

Date & Walnut Cinnamon Bites

Ingredients:

- 3 pitted medjool dates
- Ground cinnamon , to taste
- 3 walnut halves

Directions:

1. Carefully cut each walnut half into three slices, then do the same with the dates. Place a slice of walnut on top of each date, dust with cinnamon and serve.

Red Chicory, Pear & Hazelnut Salad

Ingredients:

- a good handful of rocket leaves

- 25g hazelnuts , toasted and chopped

- 2 heads of red chicory , or white if not available

- 2 ripe red Williams pears

For the dressing

- 2 tbsp mild salad oil, such as sunflower oil or safflower oil

- 1 tsp sherry or cider vinegar

- 1 tsp green peppercorns in brine, optional

- 2 tbsp hazelnut or olive oil

Directions:

1. Make the dressing. If using green peppercorns, lightly crush them in a bowl with a wooden spoon, or use a pestle and mortar.
2. Mix in the oils and vinegar and add salt to taste.
3. Trim away the chicory stalk ends and discard any limp or tired outer leaves. Carefully separate the leaves and arrange 5-6 on 4 plates if they are big, cut or tear each one into pieces.
4. Remove the stalks from the pears and quarter the pears lengthways. Cut out the cores, then thinly slice the fruit.
5. Arrange the pear slices on top of the chicory leaves and spoon over half the dressing.
6. Pour the remaining dressing over the rocket and season with salt and pepper.
7. Give the leaves a quick toss and pile on top of each salad. Sprinkle with the nuts and serve.

Easy Grilled Salmon

Ingredients:

- 300g small brown lentils , such as Castelluccio or Puy

- 2 garlic cloves , peeled

- 2 sprigs of sage (8-10 leaves)

- 6 tbsp extra-virgin olive oil

- 4 lemons

- 16 salted anchovies , rinsed, filleted and dried

- extra-virgin olive oil , for drizzling

- 8 tbsp capers , well rinsed

- 6 tbsp finely chopped fresh flat leaf parsley

- 1 side of wild salmon , from a 3.5kg/7lb 8oz fish, cut into 8, 175/6oz portions

- For the lentils

Directions:

1. Get the lentils ready first. Tip them into a small saucepan, cover with water and add the garlic and sage.
2. Simmer gently for 15-20 minutes until tender. Drain, discard garlic and sage, season with salt and pepper. Stir in olive oil and set aside.
3. Squeeze the juice of one lemon over anchovies in a bowl, add freshly ground black pepper and drizzle with olive oil.
4. Mix capers with the parsley in another bowl. You can get to here several hours in advance.
5. Preheat griddle pan until very hot. Season salmon on both sides, then sear, skin-side down (if pan is very hot the skin won't stick this goes for grilling on a barbecue, too). Turn fish over when you see it change colour halfway, then sear the other side.

6. This will take 2-3 minutes on each side for rare salmon, but cooking time may vary if pieces of fish are very thick.
7. To serve, reheat the lentils and put a large spoonful in the centre of warmed plates. Top with the salmon, skin-side up, then scatter the anchovies, capers and parsley on top. Serve with the remaining lemons.

Kidney Bean Mole With Potato Backed

Ingredients:

- Cup 7/8 (190 g) canned-cut tomatoes

- 1 tablespoon of brown sugar

- 1/3 cup (50 g) red bell pepper, cored, trimmed seeds and chopped roughly

- Vegetable stock: 5/8 cup (150ml)

- 1 table litre of cocoa powder

- 1 sesame seeds in tablespoon

- 2 teaspoons of peanut butter (smooth if available, but strong chunky)

- 7/8 cup (150 g) of frozen reindeer

- 1/4 cup (40 g) red, finely chopped onion

- 1 teaspoon of fresh ginger, finely chopped

- 2 cloves of garlic, finely chopped

- 1 thai chili, finely chopped

- 1 cup of extra virgin olive oil

- 1 teaspoon of turmeric powder

- 1 teaspoon cumin in the ground

- Pinch of clove at ground

- Pinch of cinnamon

- 1 medium potto baker

- 2 tablespoons (5 g) of chopped parsley

Directions:

1. Heat up the oven to 200oC (400 ° F).
2. In a medium saucepan, fry the onion, ginger , garlic and chili in the oil over medium heat for about 10 minutes, or until soft. Remove the

seasoning and finish cooking for another 1 to 2 minutes.
3. Place the potato on a baking tray in the hot oven and bake until soft in the middle (or longer depending on how crispy you like the outside) for 45 to 60 minutes.
4. In the meantime, add to the casserole the tomatoes, sugar, red pepper, stock, cocoa powder, sesame seeds, peanut butter, and kidney beans and cook gently for 45 to 60 min.
5. To finish sprinkle with the parsley. Break the potato in two, then pour the mole over it.

Omelet-Sirtfood

Ingredients:

- 1 Turmeric Tablespoon

- 1 cup of extra virgin olive oil

- About 2 ounces (50 g) streaky sliced bacon (or 2 rashers, smoked or regular, depending on your taste)

- 3 Medium-sized Eggs

- 11/4 ounces (35 g) red, thinly sliced endive

- 2 Table cubits (5 g) of parsley, finely chopped

Directions:

1. Heat up a frying pan with a nonstick. Cut the bacon into thin strips and cook until it is crispy over high heat.

2. You don't need to add any oil, the bacon contains enough fat for cooking. Remove from the oven, and put any extra fat on a paper towel. Wipe clean cup.
3. Whisk the eggs and mix the endive, the parsley and the turmeric together. Cut the cooked bacon into cubes, and stir in the eggs.
4. In the frying pan, heat the oil-the pan should be hot but not smoking.
5. Add the egg mixture, and move it around the pan using a spatula to start cooking the egg.
6. Keep the fried egg bits going, and rotate around the pan until the omelet number is even.
7. Reduce heat, and allow the omelet to firm. Ease the spatula around the edges and fold in half the omelet, or roll up and serve.

Baked Breast Chicken With Walnut And Parsley Pesto And Red Onion Salad

Ingredients:

- 3 spoonfuls (50ml) of water

- 5 1/2 ounces (150 g) skinless breast of chicken

- 1/8 cup (20 g) of red, finely sliced onions

- 1 Tablespoon of red wine,

- 1 1/4 ounces Arugula (35 g)

- Cherry tomatoes, 2/3 cup (100 g), half cut

- Petersil: 3/8 cup (15 g)

- 1/8 Cup Walnuts (15 g)

- 4 Parmesan cheese spoonfuls (15 g), rubbed

- 1 litre, extra virgin olive oil

- 1/2 lemon juice

- 1 Balsamic vinegar in tablespoon

Directions:

1. To make the pesto, put the parsley, walnuts, parmesan, olive oil, half the lemon juice, and a little water in a food processor or blender and mix until a smooth paste is in place. Gradually add more water until you get the consistency you prefer.
2. In the refrigerator, marinate the chicken breast in 1 tablespoon of pesto and the remaining lemon juice for 30 minutes, longer if possible.
3. Preheat to 400oF (200oC) on burner.
4. Heat a frying pan which is ovenproof over medium to high heat. In its marinade, fry the chicken on either side for 1 minute, then transfer the saucepan to the oven and cook for 8 minutes or until cooked.

5. Marinate the onions for 5 to 10 minutes in a red wine vinegar. Drain gas.
6. When cooked, remove the chicken from the oven, spoon another tablespoon of pesto over it, and let the chicken heat melt the pesto. Cover with foil and leave for 5 minutes to rest before serving.
7. Combine the balsamic vinegar with the arugula, tomatoes, and onion and drizzle. Serve with the chicken and spoon over the pesto left over.

Honey, Garlic And Chilli Oven-Roasted Squash

Ingredients:

- 4 entire garlic cloves, delicately squashed
- 5 red or green chilies, cut down the center
- 2 branches thyme
- 3 Tbsp (15 ml) honey
- 2 twig rosemary
- 1 kg grouped squash and pumpkin (no less than five unique sorts), cut in medium size pieces
- 3 Tbsp (15 ml) olive oil
- Salt and pepper to taste

Directions:

1. Preheat the stove to 300°F.

2. Take an enormous bowl and add al the fixings and permit to represent 30 minutes, blending occasionally.
3. In a simmering plate, place the Squash and cover with foil. Broil covered at 300°F for 10 minutes.
4. Increase the temperature of the broiler to 350°F, eliminate the foil, and meal for an additional 10 minutes to permit the Squash to caramel lightly.

Homemade Roasted Celery Hummus

Ingredients:

- 1 ouncefresh lime or lemon juice

- 5 stems of celery, managed and cut into 1 cm pieces (around 8 ounce) Five tablespoons olive oil (ideally EV)

- 2 pods of garlic

- 0.166 ounce salt or to taste

- 2 green serrano stew, minced

- 8 ounce cooked chickpeas

- 1/3 cup tahini

- 0.5 ounce minced parsley

Directions:

1. Place the celery into a baking platter.
2. Top with two spoonfuls of oil Place the two garlic units in a plate corner, and disperse with the bean stew. Heat at 350°F for 45 minutes in an oven.
3. Put the chickpeas into the mixer.
4. Carry some excess oil into the blender, in the hot simmered celery and other vegetables.
5. Add tahini, lime or lemon squeeze, salt, and blend until light and smooth for 3-4 minutes.
6. Remove from the blender into a bowl, add the leftover 1.5 ounce of olive oil and hacked parsley.

Kale Scramble

Ingredients:

- 1 tablespoon water
- 2 teaspoons olive oil
- 1 cup fresh kale, tough ribs removed and chopped
- 4 eggs
- 1/8 teaspoon ground turmeric
- Salt and ground black pepper, as required

Directions:

1. In a bowl, place eggs, turmeric, salt, black pepper and water and with a whisk, beat until foamy.

2. In a wok, heat the oil over medium heat. Stir in the egg mixture and immediately, reduce the heat to medium-low.
3. Cook for about 1-2 minutes, stirring frequently.
4. Stir in the kale and cook for about 3-4 minutes, stirring frequently. Remove the wok from heat and serve immediately.

Eggs With Kale

Ingredients:

- ½ pound fresh kale, tough ribs removed and chopped
- 1 teaspoon ground cumin
- ¼ teaspoon red pepper flakes, crushed
- Salt and ground black pepper, as required
- 4 eggs
- 2 tablespoons olive oil
- 1 red onion, chopped
- 2 garlic cloves, minced
- 1 cup tomatoes, chopped
- 2 tablespoons fresh parsley, chopped

Directions:

1. Heat the oil in a large wok over medium heat and sauté the onion for about 4-5 minutes.
2. Add garlic and sauté for about 1 minute. Add the tomatoes, spices, salt and black pepper and cook for about 2-3 minutes, stirring frequently.
3. Stir in the kale and cook for about 4-5 minutes.
4. Carefully, crack eggs on top of kale mixture. With the lid, cover the wok and cook for about 10 minutes or until desired doneness of eggs.
5. Serve hot with the garnishing of parsley.

Green Smoothie With Berries

Ingredients:

- 2 tsp honey
- 1 cup freshly made green Tea (dissolve honey first in Tea then chill)
- 6 ice cubes
- 1 ripe banana
- ½ cup blackcurrants (take off stems)
- 10 baby kale leaves (take off stems)

Directions:

1. Dissolve the honey in the Tea before you chill it.
2. Cool first, and then blend all the Ingredients::in the blender until smooth.
3. Serve chilled.

Green Smoothie With Grapefruit

Ingredients:

- 1 green or red apple, cored and destemmed.
- 1 carrot
- ½ cup of water (may use more or less for the texture that you like)
- 1 grapefruit, peeled and deseeded
- 6 large kale leaves, destemmed

Directions:

1. Place everything into a blender, and blend until smooth.
2. Add water if needed.
3. Serve immediately or slightly chilled

Cacao Protein Shake

Ingredients:

- Cacao powder 1 tablespoon
- 2 green apple (cored and chopped)
- Pea protein powder 3 tablespoons
- Water 2 cup
- Medjool date 2 (pitted)
- Ice five cubes
- Cinnamon powder 1 tablespoon

Directions:

1. Combine the dates, cinnamon powder, green apple, protein powder, green apple, and water in a blender and puree until well smooth.

2. Then add the ice cubes and blend again until the mixture turns thick. Serve immediately!

Power Green Smoothie

Ingredients:

- Little gem lettuce or romaine hearts one (roughly chopped)

- Ice 4 cubes (optional)

- Medjool dates two (pitted)

- Almond milk two cups

- Baby spinach one cup (chopped)

Directions:

1. Mix all your Ingredients::in a blender and puree on high speed until smooth. Serve immediately!

Sour Cherry Skyr Bowl With Kiwi And Raspberry

Ingredients:

- 30 g raspberries (fresh)

- ½ kiwi

- 1 tsp coconut rasps

- 1 tsp chia seeds

- 50 g tender oatmeal

- 30 ml Montmorency sour cherries cherry plus concentrate

- 100 g skyr nature reduced fat

- 1 shot oat drink (oat milk)

- 1 tbsp cashew butter (natural, unsweetened)

Directions:

1. Put 100 g Skyr in a bowl and mix it with a dash of oat milk until it has a yoghurt-like consistency. Stir 30 ml of Cherry PLUS sour cherry concentrate into the mixture until it has turned a light pink colour.
2. Pour 50g oat flakes, 1 teaspoon coconut flakes and 1 teaspoon chia seeds in rows over the mixture.
3. Peel and quarter ½ kiwi fruit and wash 30 g raspberries thoroughly. Garnish with fruits.
4. Finally, drizzle over 1 teaspoon of cashew butter. Serve and enjoy.

Beetroot Bread With Nasturtium

Ingredients:

- 120 g cooked beetroot (shrink-wrapped; peeled)
- salt
- 2 nasturtium flowers
- 6 sheets nasturtium
- 80 g whole rye bread (2 slices)
- 2 tsp grated horseradish (glass)

Directions:

1. Wash nasturtium leaves and shake dry.
2. Brush the bread slices with 1 teaspoon horseradish each.
3. Drain the beetroot, pat dry with kitchen paper and cut into fine slices or strips.

4. Top the slices of bread with beetroot and cress leaves. Salt lightly and arrange with the cress flowers.

Zebra Bread With Cream Cheese

Ingredients:

- 1 tsp paprika powder (sweet)
- 6 slices pumpernickel
- ½ Bundle chives
- 175 g cream cheese (13% fat)
- Salt
- Pepper

Directions:

1. Wash the chives, shake them dry and cut them into fine rolls.
2. Mix the cream cheese with a little salt and pepper. Divide into 2 portions.
3. Mix 1 portion with chives. Season the remaining cream cheese with paprika powder.

4. Spread 2 slices of Pumpernickel thick with the cream cheese mix.
5. Put 1 chive and paprika bread on top of each other. Place the remaining pumpernickel discs on top and press well.
6. Fix the loaves with 6 toothpicks each at an even distance and cut into 2 x 6 cubes.

Strawberry Buckwheat Tabbouleh

Ingredients:

- 1/8 cup of Medjool dates (pitted)
- 2 tablespoon of ground turmeric
- 2 tablespoon of capers
- 3/8 cup of tomato
- 1/3 cup of buckwheat
- Half lemon juice
- 2/3 cup of strawberries (hulled)
- 1 cup of avocado
- 2 tablespoon of extra-virgin olive oil
- 3/4 cup of parsley
- 1/8 cup of red onion

- 2-ounce arugula

Directions:

1. Cook the buckwheat with the remaining turmeric teaspoon according to product Directions:. Remove water and then put aside to let cool.
2. Afterwards, finely chop the tomato, parsley, dates, capers, red onion and avocado and then mix with the cooked buckwheat.
3. Also slice the strawberries and carefully mix into the salad with the lemon juice and oil. Serve on a bed of arugula to enjoy.

Sirtfood Green Juice

Ingredients:

- 2 big handfuls kale
- 1 to One-inch piece of fresh ginger
- 1 lemon juice
- 1 medium green apple
- 2 big handful arugula
- 1 level teaspoon matcha powder
- 2 to Three large celery stalks (including leaves)
- 1 very small handful flat-leaf parsley

Directions:

1. Mix the parsley, kale and arugula together, juice them well enough afterwards before moving to other Ingredients:.

2. The aim is to get about 2 fluid ounces or close to 1⁄4 cup of the juice.
3. At this time juice the apple, ginger and celery.
4. Peel the lemon and maybe put it through the juicer although it is easier to just squeeze gently the lemon by hand into the juice. At this phase, you should have about one cup of juice or just a little more.
5. You add the matcha when the juice is ready to be served. In a glass pour a little quantity of juice, and then add the matcha, stir strongly using a teaspoon or fork.
6. As soon as the matcha gets dissolved, add the rest of the juice. Stir one more time, and then enjoy the drink. Top with plain water or just as you desire.

Turmeric Chicken & Kale Salad With Honey Lime Dressing

Ingredients:

For the Chicken:

- Half medium brown onion (diced)

- 2 teaspoon of ghee or one tablespoon of coconut oil

- 1 lime juice

- 2 teaspoon of lime zest

- 10-ounces chicken mince or diced up chicken thighs

- 2 large garlic clove (finely diced)

- 1 teaspoon of salt plus pepper

- 2 teaspoon of turmeric powder

For the salad:

- 7 broccolini stalks or Two cups of broccoli florets
- 2 tablespoons pumpkin seeds (pepitas)
- 2 handful of fresh coriander leaves, chopped
- 2 handful of fresh parsley leaves (chopped)
- 4 large kale leaves (stems removed & chopped)
- 1 avocado (sliced)

For the dressing:

- 1 teaspoon of sea salt plus pepper

- 1 teaspoon of wholegrain or Dijon mustard

- 4 tablespoons of extra-virgin olive oil

- 2 small garlic clove, finely diced or grated

- 4 tablespoons of lime juice

- 2 teaspoon of raw honey

Directions:

1. Heat up or coconut oil or the ghee in a clean small frying pan over medium to high heat.
2. Add the onion and then sauté on medium heat for four to five minutes, until it appears golden.
3. Add the garlic and chicken mince and then stir for two to three mins over medium to high heat, breaking it away from each other.

4. Add the lime zest, turmeric, pepper, salt and lime juice and then cook, frequently stirring, for an additional three to four mins. Put aside the cooked mince.
5. As the chicken is cooking, bring a clean small saucepan of water to boil. Add the broccolini and then cook for two mins.
6. Afterwards, rinse under cold water and also cut into about three to four pieces each.
7. Add the pumpkin seeds carefully to the frying pan from the chicken and then toast over medium heat for 2 mins, frequently stirring to avoid burning. Season with some salt. Put away. You can use raw pumpkin seeds too.
8. Place the chopped kale in a clean salad bowl and then pour over the dressing. Toss and massage the kale using your hands with the dressing. It will soften the kale.

9. Lastly toss through the broccolini, fresh herbs, cooked chicken, avocado slices and pumpkin seeds.

Buckwheat Noodles With Chicken Kale

Ingredients:
For the noodles

- 1 brown onion, finely diced

- 1 medium free-range chicken breast, sliced or diced

- 1 long red chilli, thinly sliced (seeds in or out depending on how hot you like it)

- 2 large garlic cloves, finely diced

- 2-3 tablespoons Tamari sauce (gluten-free soy sauce)

- 2-3 handfuls of kale leaves (removed from the stem and roughly cut)

- 150 g / 5 oz buckwheat noodles (100% buckwheat, no wheat)

- 3-4 shiitake mushrooms, sliced

- 1 teaspoon coconut oil or ghee

For the miso dressing

- 1 tablespoon extra-virgin olive oil

- 1 tablespoon lemon or lime juice

- 1 teaspoon sesame oil (optional)

- 1½ tablespoon fresh organic miso

- 1 tablespoon Tamari sauce

Directions:

1. Bring a medium saucepan of water to boil. Add the kale and cook for 1 minute, until slightly wilted.

2. Remove and set aside but reserve the water and bring it back to the boil.
3. Add the soba noodles and cook according to the package Directions:(usually about 5 minutes). Rinse under cold water and set aside.
4. In the meantime, pan fry the shiitake mushrooms in a little ghee or coconut oil (about a teaspoon) for 2-3 minutes, until lightly browned on each side. Sprinkle with sea salt and set aside.
5. In the same frying pan, heat more coconut oil or ghee over medium-high heat. Sauté onion and chilli for 2-3 minutes and then add the chicken pieces.
6. Cook 5 minutes over medium heat, stirring a couple of times, then add the garlic, tamari sauce and a little splash of water.
7. Cook for a further 2-3 minutes, stirring frequently until chicken is cooked through.

8. Finally, add the kale and soba noodles and toss through the chicken to warm up.
9. Mix the miso dressing and drizzle over the noodles right at the end of cooking, this way you will keep all those beneficial probiotics in the miso alive and active.

Stir-Fry With Buckwheat Noodles

Ingredients:

- 1 garlic clove, finely chopped

- 1 bird's eye chilli, finely chopped 1 tsp finely chopped fresh ginger

- 20g red onions, sliced

- 40g celery, trimmed and sliced

- 75g green beans, chopped

- 50g kale, roughly chopped

- 100ml chicken stock

- 150g shelled raw king prawns, deveined

- 2 tsp tamari (you can use soy sauce if you are not avoiding gluten)

- 2 tsp extra virgin olive oil

- 75g soba (buckwheat noodles)
- 5g lovage or celery leaves

Directions:

1. Heat a frying pan over a high heat, then cook the prawns in 1 teaspoon of the tamari and 1 teaspoon of the oil for 2–3 minutes.
2. Transfer the prawns to a plate. Wipe the pan out with kitchen paper, as you're going to use it again.
3. Cook the noodles in boiling water for 5–8 minutes or as directed on the packet. Drain and set aside.
4. Meanwhile, fry the garlic, chilli and ginger, red onion, celery, beans and kale in the remaining oil over a medium–high heat for 2–3 minutes.
5. Add the stock and bring to the boil, then simmer for a minute or two, until the vegetables are cooked but still crunchy.

6. Add the prawns, noodles and lovage/celery leaves to the pan, bring back to the boil then remove from the heat and serve.

Baked Salmon Salad With Creamy Mint Dressing- Sirtfood Recipes

Ingredients:

- 2 radishes, trimmed and thinly sliced
- 5cm piece (50g) cucumber, cut into chunks
- 2 spring onions, trimmed and sliced
- 1 small handful (10g) parsley, roughly chopped
- 1 salmon fillet (130g)
- 40g mixed salad leaves
- 40g young spinach leaves

For the dressing:

- 1 tbsp natural yogurt
- 1 tbsp rice vinegar

- 2 leaves mint, finely chopped

- 1 tsp low-fat mayonnaise

- Salt and freshly ground black pepper

Directions:

1. Preheat the oven to 200°C (180°C fan/Gas 6).
2. Place the salmon fillet on a baking tray and bake for 16–18 minutes until just cooked through. Remove from the oven and set aside.
3. The salmon is equally nice hot or cold in the salad. If your salmon has skin, simply cook skin side down and remove the salmon from the skin using a fish slice after cooking. It should slide off easily when cooked.
4. 3 In a small bowl, mix together the mayonnaise, yogurt, rice wine vinegar, mint leaves and salt and pepper together and leave to stand for at least 5 minutes to allow the flavors to develop.

5. Arrange the salad leaves and spinach on a serving plate and top with the radishes, cucumber, spring onions and parsley. Flake the cooked salmon onto the salad and drizzle the dressing over.

Chargrilled Beef With A Red Wine Jus, Onion Rings, Garlic Kale And Herb Roasted Potatoes

Ingredients:

- 50g kale, sliced

- 1 garlic clove, finely chopped

- 120–150g x 3.5cm-thick beef fillet steak or 2cm-thick sirloin steak

- 40ml red wine

- 150ml beef stock

- 1 tsp tomato purée

- 100g potatoes, peeled and cut into 2cm dice

- 1 tbsp extra virgin olive oil

- 5g parsley, finely chopped

- 50g red onion, sliced into rings

- 1 tsp cornflour, dissolved in 1 tbsp water

Directions:

1. Heat the oven to 220ºC/gas 7.
2. Place the potatoes in a saucepan of boiling water, bring back to the boil and cook for 4–5 minutes, then drain.
3. Place in a roasting tin with 1 teaspoon of the oil and roast in the hot oven for 35–45 minutes.
4. Turn the potatoes every 10 minutes to ensure even cooking. When cooked, remove from the oven, sprinkle with the chopped parsley and mix well.
5. Fry the onion in 1 teaspoon of the oil over a medium heat for 5–7 minutes, until soft and nicely caramelised.
6. Keep warm. Steam the kale for 2–3 minutes then drain.
7. Fry the garlic gently in ½ teaspoon of oil for 1 minute, until soft but not coloured. Add the

kale and fry for a further 1–2 minutes, until tender. Keep warm.

8. Heat an ovenproof frying pan over a high heat until smoking. Coat the meat in ½ a teaspoon of the oil and fry in the hot pan over a medium–high heat according to
9. how you like your meat done.If you like your meat medium it would be better to sear the meat and then transfer the pan to an oven set at 220ºC/gas 7 and finish the cooking that way for the prescribed times.
10. Remove the meat from the pan and set aside to rest.
11. Add the wine to the hot pan to bring up any meat residue. Bubble to reduce the wine by half, until syrupy and with a concentrated flavor.
12. Add the stock and tomato purée to the steak pan and bring to the boil, then add the cornflour paste to thicken your sauce, adding

it a little at a time until you have your desired consistency.

13. Stir in any of the juices from the rested steak and serve with the roasted potatoes, kale, onion rings and red wine sauce.

Kale And Blackcurrant Smoothie

Ingredients:

- 1 ripe banana
- 40 g blackcurrants, washed and stalks removed
- 6 ice cubes
- 2 tsp honey
- 1 cup freshly made green tea
- 10 baby kale leaves, stalks removed

Directions:

1. Stir the honey into the warm green tea until dissolved.
1. Whiz all the ingredients together in a blender until smooth. Serve immediately.

Eggplant Salsa

Ingredients:

- 2 tsps. capers
- 6 oz. green olives, pitted and sliced
- 4 garlic cloves, minced
- 2 tsps. balsamic vinegar
- 1 tbsp. basil, chopped
- 1 ½ c. tomatoes, chopped
- 3 c. eggplant, cubed
- A drizzle of olive oil
- Black pepper to the taste

Directions:

1. Heat up a pan with the oil over medium-high heat, add eggplant, stir and cook for 5 minutes.
2. Add tomatoes, capers, olives, garlic, vinegar, basil and black pepper, toss, cook for 5 minutes more, divide into small cups and serve cold.
3. Enjoy!

Carrots And Cauliflower Spread

Ingredients:

- 1 c. almond milk
- 1 tsp. garlic powder
- ¼ tsp. smoked paprika
- 1 c. carrots, sliced
- 2 c. cauliflower florets
- ½ c. cashews
- 2 ½ c. water

Directions:

1. In a small pot, mix the carrots with cauliflower, cashews and water, stir, cover, bring to a boil over medium heat, cook for 40 minutes, drain and transfer to a blender.

2. Add almond milk, garlic powder and paprika, pulse well, divide into small bowls and serve
3. Enjoy!

Italian Veggie Salsa

Ingredients:

- 2 tbsps. olive oil
- A pinch black pepper
- 1 tsp. Italian seasoning
- 2 red bell peppers, cut into medium wedges
- 3 zucchinis, sliced
- ½ c. garlic, minced

Directions:

1. Heat up a pan with the oil over medium-high heat, add bell peppers and zucchini, toss and cook for 5 minutes.
2. Add garlic, black pepper and Italian seasoning, toss, cook for 5 minutes more, divide into small cups and serve as a snack. Enjoy!

Smoked Salmon Omelet

Ingredients:

- 1 ¼ cups chopped arugula
- 2 teaspoons chopped parsley
- 1 teaspoon olive oil for cooking
- 4 medium eggs
- 1 1/3 cups sliced smoked salmon
- 1 teaspoon capers

Directions:

1. Crack up the eggs into a bowl and combine. You must whisk well until well mixed.
2. Add all Ingredients::to the egg and mix well to combine.

3. Heat your olive oil in a frying pan until hot and shimmering, but not smoking on medium-high heat
4. Add the mixture to the pan and use your spatula to spread it evenly throughout
5. Reduce the heat to medium and wait for the omelet to complete cooking
6. When finished, use your spatula to roll or fold the omelet.

Cheesy Baked Eggs

Ingredients:

- 1 tablespoon parsley
- ½ teaspoon ground turmeric
- 1 tablespoon olive oil
- 4 large eggs
- 75 grams (3 ounces) cheese, grated
- 25 grams (1 ounce) fresh rocket (arugula) leaves, finely chopped

Directions:

1. Grease each ramekin dish with a little olive oil.
2. Divide the rocket (arugula) between the ramekin dishes, then break an egg into each one.

3. Sprinkle a little parsley and turmeric on top, then sprinkle on the cheese.
4. Place the ramekins in a preheated oven at 220ºC/425ºF for 15 minutes until the eggs are set and the cheese is bubbling.

Oatmeal Banana Pancakes With Walnuts

Ingredients:

- 1/8 cup chopped walnuts

- ¼ cup old-fashioned oats

- 1 finely diced firm banana

- 1 cup whole-wheat pancake mix

Directions:

1. Make the pancake mix according to the Directions:on the package.
2. Add walnuts, oats, and chopped banana.
3. Coat a skillet with cooking spray.
4. Add about ¼ cup of the pancake batter onto the griddle when hot.
5. Turn pancake over when bubbles form on top. Cook until golden brown.
6. Serve immediately.

Buckwheat And Strawberries Salad

Ingredients:

- 20 g red onion
- 25 g Medjool dates, pitted
- 1 tbsp. capers
- 30 g parsley
- 100 g strawberries, hulled
- 1 tbsp. extra virgin olive oil juice of
- 1/2 lemon
- 50 g buckwheat
- 1 tbsp. ground Tumeric
- 80 g avocado
- 65 g tomato

- 30 g rocket

Directions:

1. Cook the buckwheat with the turmeric according to the packet Directions:. Drain and keep to one side to cool.
2. Chop the tomato, red onion, avocado, dates, parsley, and capers and mix with the cool buckwheat.
3. Slice the strawberries and gently blend the oil and lemon juice into the salad. Serve on a bed of rocket.

Miso And Sesame Glazed Tofu With Ginger And Chili Stir-Fried Greens

Ingredients:

- 2 courgette, sliced thin
- 3 bird's eye chili, seeds removed and finely chopped (optional as quite spicy)

- 3 garlic cloves, finely chopped
- 3 teaspoons fresh ginger, finely chopped Four teaspoon sesame seeds
- 100g (1 1/4 cup) kale, washed and chopped 235 ml (1 cup) water
- 70g (1/2cup) buckwheat or buckwheat noodles Two teaspoon ground turmeric
- 5 teaspoons extra virgin olive oil
- 2 tablespoon mirin
- 2 tablespoons (40g) brown miso paste
- 250g firm tofu
- 2 stick of celery, trimmed, stringy pieces peeled away and chopped finely
- 2 red onion, sliced thin
- 3 teaspoon tamari

Directions:

1. Preheat your oven to 200°C/gas 6
2. Line a small roasting tin with parchment or greaseproof paper.
3. Mix the miso and mirin together in a bowl. Cut the tofu, then cut each piece in half, forming triangles.
4. With the miso mixture, cover the tofu and leave to marinate as you are preparing the other Ingredients:.
5. Cook the kale in a steamer for five minutes, remove it and leave it on one side. Place a pan of water on the hob and bring to a rolling boil; place a collider over the top of the kale; this will serve as a steamer if you don't have one.
6. Slice the trimmed celery, red onion, and courgette in the corner while the kale is cooking.

7. Then the chili (making sure all seeds are removed), garlic, and ginger are thinly chopped and left on one side.
8. In the roasting pan, put the marinated tofu, sprinkle the sesame seeds over the tofu, and roast for twenty minutes until nicely caramelized.
9. Wash the buckwheat in a sieve and boil a cup of water, adding the turmeric and a pinch of salt to taste.
10. Attach the buckwheat and leave it on high heat until the water has started boiling.
11. When buckwheat has expanded and started to absorb the water, reduce to low heat, and put the lid on, cook for fifteen minutes. The buckwheat is cooked once all the water has been absorbed.
12. Heat the olive oil in a frying pan when the tofu has 5 minutes left, heat the olive oil in a frying pan, when hot add the courgette, chili, celery,

onion, ginger, and garlic and fry on high heat for two minutes, then reduce to medium heat for four minutes until the vegetables are cooked through but still crunchy.

13. You will need to add a tablespoon of water if the vegetables start to stick to the pan. Add the tamari and kale and cook for another minute.
14. Serve with the greens and buckwheat when the tofu is ready.

Buckwheat Noodles

Ingredients:

- 1 chopped fresh ginger
- 1 freshly chopped bird's eye chili
- Chicken stock, 100 ml
- Sliced red onions, ½ cup
- Chopped kale, ½ cup
- Sliced and trimmed celery, ½ cup
- Celery leaves or lovage, 1 tsp
- Shrimps, deveined and shelled, 1 ½ cup
- Extra virgin olive oil, 2 tsp
- Buckwheat noodles, 1 cup
- Soy sauce or tamari (gluten-free), 2 tsp

- 1 chopped garlic clove
- Chopped green beans, 1 cup

Directions:

1. Cook shrimps with 1 tsp of soy sauce or tamari and 1 tsp of olive oil for a couple of minutes on high heat.
2. Pour the prawns out of the pan and wipe down oil residue with kitchen paper.
3. Cook buckwheat noodles for up to eight minutes, drain and leave on the side to cool off.
4. As your noodles cool down, fry the remaining Ingredients::(kale, beans, celery, ginger, red onion, chili, and garlic) up to three minutes.
5. Add the stock to the mix and simmer for a couple more minutes.
6. The vegetables should be cooked but still fresh-looking and crunchy.

7. Finally, add the buckwheat noodles, celery, and prawns to the pan, boil briefly, and you're done.

Baked Oatmeal

Ingredients:

- 2 cups unsweetened almond milk or 2% milk

- 1 cup low-fat plain Greek yogurt

- ¼ cup unadulterated maple syrup

- 3 tablespoons extra-virgin olive oil

- 2 teaspoon vanilla concentrate

- 3 pears, diced at least

- 2 cups old-fashioned oats

- ½ cup pecans, hacked

- 2 teaspoons ground cinnamon

- 2 teaspoon preparing powder

- ¾ teaspoon salt

- ¼ teaspoon ground nutmeg

- ⅛ teaspoon ground cloves

- ⅓ cup low-fat plain Greek yogurt

Directions:

1. Preheat stove to 375 degrees F. Coat a 9-inch-square preparing dish with cooking shower.
2. Blend oats, pecans, cinnamon, heating powder, salt, nutmeg, and cloves in a huge bowl. Whisk almond milk (or milk), 1 cup yogurt, syrup, oil, and vanilla In a medium bowl.
3. Empty the wet fixings into the dry fixings. Delicately blend in. Move the blend to the readied heating dish.
4. Heat until brilliant darker, 45 to 55 minutes.

Choc Chip Granola

Ingredients:

- 1 tbsp dull dark colored sugar
- 2 tbsp rice malt syrup
- 60g high quality (70%) flat chocolate chips
- 200g gigantic oats
- 50g walnuts, generally cleaved
- 3 tbsp light olive oil
- 20g spread

Directions:

1. Preheat the stove to 160°C (140°C fan/Gas 3). Line a substantial preparing plate with a silicone sheet or heating material.
2. Mix the oats and walnuts In a large bowl. In at least nonstick dish, tenderly warmth the

vegetable oil, spread, dark colored sugar, and rice malt syrup until the margarine has liquefied and therefore the sugar and syrup have choppy. Try not to permit to bubble.

3. Pour the syrup over the oats and blend all until the oats are completely secured.
4. Distribute the granola over the preparing plate, spreading directly into the corners.
5. Leave clusters of blend with dispersing rather than a good spread. Heat In the grill for 20 minutes until just tinged brilliant dark colored at the sides. Take it far from the stove and leave to chill on the plate.
6. When cold, separate any longer significant irregularities on the plate together with your fingers and afterward blend In the chocolate chips.
7. Scoop or empty the granola into a sealed shut tub or container. The granola will keep for in any event fortnight.

Caramelized Cauliflower

Ingredients:

- 2 tbl   extra virgin olive oil (plus oil for coating the baking sheet)
- 1/4 tsp salt
- 1/4 tsp ground black pepper
- 3 tbl grated pecorino romano cheese
- 1 large cauliflower head cut into bite-size florets (about 8 cups)
- 1 medium red onion cut in half then across in 3/4-inch thick slices

Directions:

1. Preheat the oven to 425°F. Lightly coat a large baking sheet with oil.

2. Combine the cauliflower, onion, extra virgin olive oil, salt, and pepper in a large bowl; toss well to coat.
3. Transfer mixture to the prepared baking sheet. Roast until the cauliflower is browned and tender, 28 to 30 minutes, stirring occasionally.
4. Remove from the oven and transfer to a large bowl; stir in the cheese then pour the mixture back onto the baking sheet.
5. Return to the oven and bake 3 minutes. Serve warm or at room temperature.

Colorado Potato Hash

Ingredients:

- 1/2 cup blue cheese, crumbled
- 1/2 cup heavy cream
- Kosher salt to taste
- Ground pepper to taste
- Italian parsley, finely chopped, to taste
- 2 russet or purple potaotes
- 2 red potatoes
- 2 yukon gold potatoes
- 1/4 cup   extra virgin olive oil
- 1/2 tbl chopped fresh garlic
- 1 tbl chopped fresh shallots

- 6 slices applewood bacon, cooked and chopped

Directions:

1. Dice unpeeled potatoes into medium-sized cubes and blanch half way in boiling water.
2. Drain potatoes and rinse with cold running water until fully cooled. Toss potaotes in a small amount of oil to prevent sticking; refrigerate.
3. Heat a saute pan and add   extra virgin olive oil. Add potaotes slowly to avoid any splatter of oil, and saute for 4-5 minutes.
4. Add garlic and shallots and saute until golden brown. Add blue cheese and cook until melted.
5. Add cream and cook until reduced by three-fourths.
6. This mixture should be thick and hearty. Season as needed with salt and pepper. Garnish with chopped parsley and bacon.

www.ingramcontent.com/pod-product-compliance
Lightning Source LLC
LaVergne TN
LVHW010226070526
838199LV00062B/4737